WHIRLING
BACKWARD
INTO THE
WORLD

WHIRLING BACKWARD INTO THE WORLD

poems by
Michael Scofield

SANTA FE

On the cover: *Spring Coalescence*,
a monotype by Jan Nelson from the author's collection.

Sunstone books may be purchased for educational, business, or sales
promotional use. For information please write:
Special Markets Department, Sunstone Press,
P.O. Box 2321, Santa Fe, New Mexico 87504-2321.

Library of Congress Cataloging-in-Publication Data:

Scofield, Michael.
Whirling backward into the world : poems / by Michael Scofield.
    p. cm.
ISBN 0-86534-474-4 (pbk. : alk. paper)
I. Title.

PS3619.C63W48 2006
811'.54--dc22

                                                            2005033868

Published in

WWW.SUNSTONEPRESS.COM
SUNSTONE PRESS / POST OFFICE BOX 2321 / SANTA FE, NM 87504-2321 /USA
(505) 988-4418 / ORDERS ONLY (800) 243-5644 / FAX (505) 988-1025

for Noreen

ACKNOWLEDGMENTS

Many thanks to these journals
for first publishing the following poems,
sometimes in earlier versions:

Chokecherries: "Seeing My Father"

Cimarron Review: "Target Practice"

The Comstock Review: "Kate's Daydream" (under the title "Dream World"), "Ship in a Bottle"

Diner: "Breakup," "What His Professor Said"

Eldorado Sun: "How I Feel About You," "Why the Army Assigned Me a Psychiatrist"

Red Rock Review: "After Cryotransport, Lo," "Tightrope," "Whirling Has Worked for the Sufis Since 1273"

Rhino: "Tonight Nothing Works" (under the title "Porn Nocturne"), "War Again"

The Santa Clara Review: "Giving Up," "Overpopulation," "Soaring" (under the title "Flight"), "Today's World"

thedrunkenboat: "Affliction," "Begging His Doppelganger"

I am grateful to professors Jack Myers, Mary Ruefle, Leslie Ullman, and Roger Weingarten—and to colleagues Elly Clay and Eve Rifkah—in the Vermont College 2000-2002 low-residency MFA program, for helping me rework many of the poems that follow; and for encouragement from Santa Fe-area poets Charles Bell, Sheila Cowing, Jon Davis, Janet Eigner, Morgan Farley, Thomas Fitzsimmons, Greg Glazner, Donald Levering, Dana Levin, Richard Lehnert, James McGrath, Joan Mitchell, Carol Moldaw, Frank Moore, Mary Morris, Barbara Riley, Barbara Rockman, Arthur Sze, and Kathryn Ugoretz.

Special thanks go to Rebecca Seiferle for overseeing completion of the manuscript, to Richard Lehnert for copyediting, to Karen Bolander-Claus, Randy Freeman, and Russel Stolins for guidance in formatting, and to Vicki Ahl for art direction.

CONTENTS

GIVING UP / 45

O FRABJOUS DAY / 77

PREFACE

These poems hope to tell about the way humans are in the world: how we find ourselves out and how we manage the divide between self and others. Of course, each piece comes out my own experience, driven by love of language.

I tell my students that finding how to create energetic poetry is the best way to learn to write anything—articles, diaries, memoirs, stories, novels, even emails. But the basics of discovering how to use similes and metaphors, to wield image verbs ("She tap-danced into the bedroom" versus "She came into the bedroom"), to use touch and fragrance as well as sight, to write "He flung the cat through the window" versus "The cat was flung," to glory in the power that comes from rewriting and rewriting and rewriting is only the skeleton. More than anything, writing poetry requires a feeling that I've got to share my struggles in order to keep my spirit free of disharmony. I feel more integrated putting words on paper than doing almost anything else.

It took me a while to find my way to poetry. For decades I sold magazine advertising space and wrote how-to-do-it books for an established publisher on the West Coast. Desperate to be more creative, under a pen name I published free-lance articles in San Francisco's city, ballet, and symphony magazines, rising in the predawn to write before work. When I left the how-to publisher in 1987, my wife Noreen and I started our own home business, creating marketing documents for executives in Silicon Valley. Turning technobabble into riveting prose proved daunting— and, true, profitable. But I needed more than money to keep going at such a pace.

Consoling myself with the verbal music of poets like W.B. Yeats and Elizabeth Bishop and Hayden Carruth, I started writing my own poetry at age 53. For the first couple of years I tried sonnets and terza rima, sestinas and villanelles, pouring through Judson Jerome's *The Poet's Handbook* and Steve Kowit's *In the Palm of Your Hand—The Poet's Portable Workshop*. I attended poetry groups and workshops and began to submit work to poetry journals. Within three years, for every twenty-five poems mailed, I was getting one accepted. As astonishing, technical clients had begun to call us; more and more they loved the copy we were giving them. Soon we had more work than we could handle. How then could I bring fresh energy to my poems?

Noreen and I escaped to Santa Fe but soon each of us landed in the hospital, exhausted from years of sixty-hour workweeks. The marketing-document business had to go. After we got our health back, I resolved to devote whatever life I had left to creative writing. I earned a low-residency MFA/Writing from Vermont College—what a treasure that two-year experience continues to be—took on students, and plunged into rewriting and rewriting, poem by poem, the collection you have in your hands. May the "I" not obtrude as you read.

—*Michael Scofield*
Santa Fe

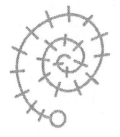

BEGGING
HIS
DOPPELGANGER

Affliction

Whether or not You are
or care—believing numbs
and salts the sting of watching the tips
of my sister's fingers crack, hearing
her voice a hunted
crow's the night she finally managed to go, pills
spilling from her hand at dinner like
daisies dotting her romaine. Did You

guide her slump
to the bathroom tiles? Was her muscle relaxant
Your holy bread?

Myself surgically split like butterflied
lamb last spring—whether cobbled together by
    grace or
thousand-dollar bills, I wince
to see the morning wind beat an Anna's hummer
back against the patio wall, battling
to reach a penstemon blossom, throat and crown
    feathers
tossing like Fra Angelico flame.

What His Professor Said

That's the wrong motif. The right motif
is birds. Canaries in a freighter's hold, peregrines
   when
soaring. Birds drop
blessings as gamblers drop
cash. If I can grab one I can feel it
throbbing. *It's not the berries*

that do the shaking. It's my heart wishing it were
anything else: a sea cucumber. Give it
padded silk and cedar slats. Bury it or dry it
until the wind makes it a kite. *High-performance*

writing gets in the way. Under-the-influence
roadblock, red blur,
lady cop's tooth
silver as her shades. Taps
on her boot heels—heart, be
a submachine gun. *Is love*

a code word here? My love is a
cassowary who this morning
rolled over
to whisper she's leaving for a man with a bad
heart loving hunting even more
than she does. *Your work is*

*bathyspheric. I can't picture why you're washing
ball bearings. Flossing's a better metaphor.*

Tightrope

He's trying not to swallow
the vinegar paste his electric toothbrush grinds
his gums with as the dentist's

drill of last night's
dream blurs his reflection like a blow
to the testicles: he couldn't

choke his dead mother into gasping I love
you as the white-headed pin she jammed

through his red carnation kept drawing
blood—two dreams ago, his past

wife tightened one of her nylons
around his throat, popping his eardrums. He drops
his robe, approaching the shower as though

its milk glass hides the wife crouching
or mother aiming
a knife on tiptoes or who knows—his soul,

a one-eyed cat needing a home.

Report from the Interior

What a vocabulary! On our

afternoon stroll Mother told me that
in the e-procurement

stew of pharmaceuticals,
rogue electrons make their own reality—

foraging ants serve as models. She demonstrated

by staggering around a bronze statue of
James D. Watson raising his cap

from a horse with a braided tail. Though I'm
　　pushing

for assisted living, she's determined
to paint her apartment and continue hosting her
　　Wednesday
soup-and-poetry soirées

since seven Nobel Laureates have advised her
not to rush into anything.

Target Practice

To stopper rage at my country's lust
to preempt, I've unfolded my chair
near the *Pray for Peace* sign skewering
the lawn that graces our state capitol.
Nearby a guy's cupping his knees and two sandaled
girls kneel on mats. How I'd love

to turn those legislators clacking up
the concrete path—chattering
into cell phones or cajoling
secretaries under the rows of pear trees—into
    pacifists
quiet as we. One who just beep-locked

his truck stares over, dress shirt festooning
his belly, sombrero cocked. Tossing
her crow-black cascade, his secretary rises
off pumps to kiss his earlobe and leads him

across the low chain, *Stay Off the Grass.*
Is that honeysuckle
she's soaked herself in? Scram
in your double-breasted gabardine, eyes
sleep-deprived—your boss's
boots unsteady our ground. As I steeple

my fingers, tuck my chin, her heel
slams my sternum and to their laughter
I'm whirling backward
into the world.

Numbed at the Memorial

Kudos to the mariachi duo of Baca and Fernandez but
   how could

the murdered's mother daze her way through joss-
   stick
fumes to kiss the fifteen-year-old

killer's shaved head

and why did she grin at us,
false teeth white buttered corn, bobbing her fresh

Grand Forks perm? And where
was the murdered's bride? The murdered himself

was ashes settled in a blue pot beside the wedding

photos as his brothers, buttoned to their
Adam's apples, pumped the killer's hand,
his long black lashes unblinking. Ballet Bob
   choreographed

four young girls to intertwine and cup each others'

chins while a woman unknown to us wailed
"Amazing Grace." Reverend Gwen praised God that
    the murdered
no longer cared

to hear his Harley. At the sharing, the murdered's
best friend Biker Billy stuttered how

he loved the killer, shifting feet
like a man needing to pee. A muscle in my thigh
    pulsed
against the pew until

a hundred of us rose to mouth the murdered's
    favorite, "Born to
be Wild" by Steppenwolf. Later, heavy-metal music
    heralding

juice and cookies

blasted the adobe of the church's education building
    but
my wife and I hurried home for ice cream. Next
    morning pain
slammed my head

as though I'd chugged a quart of Gilbey's Gin.

Basic Training

Yes, sir, sonofabitch
cocksucker. I fucked up after I fucked
around. Shut
the fuck up, you fucking

We are not an imperialist nation

yardbird. Suck
my dick, motherfucker, your teeth
shine so yellow your tongue leaps up and cries
gold rush. Spit shine, double-time, no

We're a peace-loving nation

talk. You do what when a bee parks
on your nose? "Sir, dress
to the right and cover." Give me fifteen, down
on the ground, what's the purpose

Our laws are God-given through the people

of the bayonet? "To kill." Two
kinds of bayonet warriors, the quick
and the dead, you're
what? This is my rifle, that is

When it's necessary to fight we will do so

my gun. This is for fighting, that
is for fun—horizontal
butt. Vertical butt. The slash, the
jab. I want screams when you lunge.

We have never lost a war

Soaring

Awash in Old Lyme and buttoned
in a navy blazer so they'll be proud of me, riding

the up escalator after the visit, acne
persisting and stooped from years of actuarial

calculations. Dad Sir Jackal two steps above me
Got your ticket, buddy? Mother in helmet

hairdo, squeezing his elbow against terminal
blare, smiling *What flight, honey?* Her voice

castor oil spooned down me—and I'm
in diapers again, screaming at the fingernails

yanking safety pins, Jackal's paws
cramping my ankles. *Buddy, stop it*

now, hear me? Flips me. She peels
the stinking cotton off, cold air stinging as

they step from the glint of disappearing
stairs and twist back. *That sounds like the old*

asthma, honey, but I'm humming
"Jesus Savior Pilot Me" and in minutes

I'll be—*oh, proud of me, be*
proud of me, be proud.

Attempting to Clear My Head Before Leaving the House

If I double-knot these black-and-white
bootlaces, they won't loosen

when I tramp the Winsor Trail,
yes?—last time the trick

freed me to gawk at harrier hawks
patrolling the ponderosas. My dream book

says the $21 bills I flung at cripples last night
mean earth. But why, tossing

money, did I wear
that ratty cap? The book says its

dun orange means low intellect. Having just flossed
with mint-flavored twist, I'm less

likely to bother a hiker
since when I prayed at dawn,

"Help me do Your will," the voice I call God
rattled the back of my head, "Everything is

as it should be"—the *I Ching*
quote I read yesterday. Yet I'm *wheezing* and all

I'm doing is grabbing my pack off the shelf
    watching clouds
scud through a deep blue the book

calls "awakened spiritual forces." So if I push
the door open, unless I trip I'll cross the aluminum

into a morning like yesterday's
scented with juniper, yes?

Begging His Doppelganger

In last night's dream why were you
shrouded in white linen, pleats like flutes
on a mausoleum column, head lolling
sideways, neck snapped?

Boding the end to thirty-eight years
of kissing Clara good morning, rising
to rainbow my sunken chest
in a red-yellow pullover?

This morning I pick poppies for Mother's
lap, wipe slop from her see-through
bib. Tonight Clara and I dance at the Cattlemen's
Food-for-the-Homeless Social.

Come tonight as a youth, okay? Linenless,
playing the piccolo. Say I've more time
to build self-esteem through good works.

Give Us This Day

Why did You give me this ant-swarming
mind, these burst-bladder

emotions? To send me scuttling
toward stupa, synagogue, mosque, or

cathedral—hog-tie me
in ritual? Or simply to relish my outrage

at rum bottles and needle
caps picked up on walks, my twisting

intestine when I see that bristle-headed
father jerking his daughter

toward heaven to slap her? Give thanks
for what is, is that

what You're asking? For the mother's
shrieks as well as Bach's suites

for unaccompanied cello? Forgive me, this morning
I'm cowering under the covers.

Tonight Nothing Works

He crumples his try
at a nature lyric with its insight that six

white swans illumine dark water as a newt

on the sand wriggles his skin off
like the woman here
unbuttoning her shirt—

this moment of privacy reconciling desire with the terror

of exposure. He grasps her nipple
rings and pulls her to him, tensing

his thighs like the howl
of sirens while grape hyacinths in windows exhale

a fragrance of horses
and the hairs
on her forearms flash and the flesh

of her back feels like

flesh
and her lips humming at his ear make him
sneeze like a snail fizzing

Ship in a Bottle

Square-rigger stuck in your brandy
bottle, rigging yellowed and green clay sea
vinegary when I unscrew the cap,
my belly roils as I recall my ex
hurling you into the arroyo, my eyes mist
watching our toddler, now twice divorced,
drool you across the kilim. Huddled
with you for sixty years, at last I hear
the ice pack cracking.

Agape

How can I love my Mexican hairless,
much less mankind when vertigo
and migraine stuff me
into a gunny sack and stomp it when
I struggle? Hurl chrysanthemums
of flame, petals of flesh and melting Boeings
into a mind already messed
with colonic pain, honey of halothane, rubber
gloves and knives?

Neruda says, *Now count
to twelve and just keep still for once.* A sudden
disciple, I'm startled to hear
my heartbeat rise in this small room, breathing
with others while watching the ice storm
spatter double panes of glass.

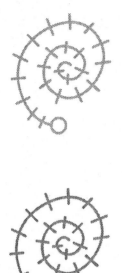

GIVING UP

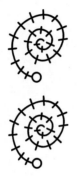

Overpopulation

You want me to take another slice
of ham? More rosé? My stomach already sounds
like the dishwasher. Next Sunday
one serving of egg salad and buttermilk
or I'm not coming over. You think

I don't love you if I don't
bolt for the toilet and why
must I praise your hundreds
of Hummel figurines? Sure, you're my ma
but I gag seeing shelf fulls
of *Alpine Dancers* ogling
squadrons of *Pretzel Boys*. I wish

you'd had just me. Did you truly
need nine? They're breeding
like fleas, Ma. I can't keep up
with the birthdays. I can't do it.

Terror

O straggle-bearded god swaddled
in leggings and blue tassled cap, reeking of burning
mugwort, cushioned
on the lawn that fronts the State Capitol—lead us in
    prayer
for world peace. Outraged by corporate
chicanery, you've turned buju, Buddhist Jew wolf
with a begging bowl
stomaching a howl of shame. You can't any longer

advocate bonds knowing General Food's chief
votes to boost his own salary
forty percent a year. While farmers' market farmers'
orchards shrivel. While Nigerians
boil weeds. Mr. Buju,

how are we to live? Surely not propped
on prayer cushions here. You'll change
your livelihood to help Santa Fe's
bracelet makers set up balance sheets? And I'm to
    return
to grunt work penning their brochures? But I'm
an investor with a liver condition, busy scribbling
    couplets
that glorify pain.

Trying to Learn to Kill

General Tooley, sir,

we're doing our best slaving
in sand whizzing like shrapnel to stay *lively*

though my head is a cracked
bell, knees soccer balls, my ears

cauliflowered by the thunderclaps of M-1s
     slamming
our shoulders, barrels jerking

like the erections we can't get

squinting at straw shimmying
in this salt haze,

BAM, targets yanked for scoring,

popping up like lollipops with pocked cheeks—
we're *working hard*

50

like you said
in service to this great

country but oh,

goddamn it,
down in the pit the noncoms are stabbing

holes in bull's-eyes with yellow pencils, scrubbing
    our scorecards
to make us look like

marksmen. Sir, I just blew

two rounds, one slug frizzed the wrong target's
    edge, another
singed a wave like those I used to ride.

Rowboats

I stopped sailing
with my preteen daughter
to the Korean teahouse
where we munched almond cakes

to pant over purchasing sequined sweaters
for the widow who gave me oral sex,
belly pouring over her thighs
like sorghum—

married, divorced her, stared for years
at the envelopes holding checks
my daughter scrawled Return to Sender.
Last week on a whim

on her twenty-first birthday I asked
a search engine

to find her number. She'd wed
a poker-loving securities lawyer
whose shirt pocket yesterday stank
of lilac. I heard the little boy

she held to the mike gurgle
Da?—heard her weep that her baby

was her rowboat. Mine is remembering
almond cakes, I said, blurting,

What's your husband, your guided-missile
deep-sea cruiser? After the silence, Good
to hear from you, Dad. Maybe we'll come
see you some day.

Why the Army Assigned Me a Psychiatrist

Before shipping to Korea, testosterone-swollen
and bristle-scalped,
we rammed bayonets into the navels
of slit-eyed scarecrows swinging from 4x4s
jammed into dunes
north of Pebble Beach Country Club, jabbering
our longing to gang-bang local
public high schoolers. But one morning,

hurling grenades toward clumps of seaweed
our sergeant had cobbled into killers,
we watched a seal's head explode off
its body, one torn flipper spin
across the breakers—and though the others cheered,
I lost my knees, crumpling to gobble quartz
as though it were grains of sugar.

A Mother's Mind Unties Its Bow

Look, blisher your necktie, straighten your drake,
and give me my moment to fake how abysmally
    thrilled
I am that you've come. But stop slurping that
    shake—

oh, gerden lissy, flower my merry-go, flurry of
    peppered orange
pittosporum, rattlesnake
over some daffodilled
snowflake,

coss. Ungash. Slacken my lashes, ratchet my
    bellyache,
slap this slobbering unfulfilled
eyesore gifting a poppycot fruitcake.
Red, blue, black, rose: fire one.

Today's World

Certainly the writer
of a newsletter for art collectors,
scratching into flame

a paper match
to sterilize the pin to lance the lump
under his nose,
would call Emergency

for his neighbor,
an art-history professor
clutching his belly—
its scar tissue

wrapping his aorta
like a starved anaconda—
if he could hear
the moans.

But their town houses share
a double-thick wall
so the writer,

having tweezed
the whisker, dabs peroxide
as the other, slack-jawed,

wrapped in his robe,
stiffens on the rug.

How Are We to Hug Now?

when you laugh that you just bought
the wife a crimson

turbocharged coupe to complete
the American flag of your blue all-wheel-drive

sunroofed van whose white wheelchair decal—
(though your new hip pivots
without a creak) privileges you to park

steps from our resolve to reheat our friendship
in this latte saloon recalling

long-ago bar stools,
our slurred
confessions, the slosh

through winters until bourbon
broke us. Rubble heaps on

rubble—you tell me latilla ceilings
and a sweep of iris primp the duplex
you've bought to rent out, cashing

stock options
before your company swandove. Not

give back your gains or lavish them
on the homeless? My false
smile spreads—soon,

soft as wrapping gauze,
I'll pitch the grenade *so you're liking Bush's rush*
to war? as you liken him
to Reagan if the economy soars,
to Milosevic if your investments veer

from leaf drift to drop—oh, let it go. Dried-out
drunk whom I need

like sneaked smokes,
let's bear hug what's left
and light up.

Seeing My Father

in this tall klutz who just tipped over
his glass of water, soaking
the folding chair, I jump
from the audience, unfolding
my handkerchief because I love his peppery
thicket of hair, long to learn the music
that turns his poems of family combat
into dance. Dear

mentor, be Abraham to my Isaac, don't
let me down like Dad who slapped
me free of hero worship then drowned
remorse in gin. You stoop

to spill, I kneel
to steady, wish Dad could have risen
or that I were your Jewish
son. When after the applause you ask me
to join you for coffee, I say no.

She Asked Me to Massage Her Dry,

he sobs,
gray-whiskered friend who'd grinned
that Julie said yes, she'd marry him

from the bath she smelled of crushed
geranium but last night's dream
dropped like a scrim, the hair
I stroked was blue as slate—Mother's, gut

ballooning   in wrinkled
gingham,   her   cigarette wheeze
pleading me
into her bed,   her   underarms
wobbling   like Father's jowls as
he rushed in

Julie asked, What's wrong, Jim?
asked me to kiss her

breasts,   but   I could only
see the gash
in Mother's rouge,   the purpling
cheek,   the ashtray Father   grabbed
to hurl again.

Night Outside the Teen Center

She thrusts toward his cupped
palm as though lusting to be
burned. As her cheeks pucker,
he takes the cigarette
from her, tosses his match, tongues
the rouge on her filter, pushes
its hot tip against a cold one she
shakes from her pack,
sucks until it glows and returns it,
mouthing the one she lit. Dear Past

with cap wrenched backward,
girl with too much rouge, how I miss
your ritual, its pornography
of what's to come—how I long
to shorten
my own life again.

How I Feel About You

Blue whales alpha-waving miles through the murk
    to scratch each other's rashes. Artichoke thistles
    entwined from puffs the wind planted. A pair of
    steepled bells: bink, bong. Sometimes our two
    rivers merge across the boulders.

Cottontail, gardenia,
dandelion, forget-me-not,
razor blade, kingfisher,
queen of hearts, snarl
of twine

"Just because you hike eight miles doesn't mean I
    can. Get in the other lane. You need to gargle.
    Charcoal doesn't go with persimmon. I can talk
    about my girlhood if I want to; I can shop for
    towels. Doesn't anyone see how unhappy I am?"

Under the comforter, Boieldieu's harp concerto
spills from the radio. I brush your shoulder
and you twist your thinness
to smooth my hair.

Still Youthful in Their Testes

They find the loan officer sexy with her rainwater
long-lashed eyes,

the two old friends who chatter like chipmunks
disputing a branch. He with stubble

on his jowls once rolled on Jamaican sand
with a girl who yanked

his trunks off. He with blotches on his scalp
recalls the pumpkin pudding he licked

off his wife's bubbies while she
sprayed him with a magnum

of champagne. As their explanations tumble out,
one sees the loan officer on all fours,

the other sniffs gardenia on the robe she's sashed
open to her navel—

until she throws a hand up. *One of you*
tell me slowly
who most qualifies
to buy this
RV you want
to hit the road in. Silence as though

she holds a mirror
to the wrinkles on their necks and upper lips.

Last Gasp

I washed into Santa Fe sickened by Silicon
Valley innovation but this morning padded
downstairs to watch my handcrafted
Santo Domingo floor tiles pop up

like tepees. My Arab broker
is an aromatherapist, my descended-
from-conquistadors banker marches his *War
Is Terrorism*

while I crisp
like a jellyfish beached under halogens
in the St. John's College Great Books library, unable
to suck up any more krill.

I'm Under a Doctor's Care Now
(That Outfit Cost a Lot)

To thirty years of marriage we spooned the last
of cherries jubilee. The maitre d'
dimmed the lights, we rose to jig to the clarinet and
    her hair

roared into flame. Shreds

of red from that white wave shimmied
toward the chandelier as drums
and bass drove the reed to fury. Pushing away,

she pirouetted, the fire braided, her silk-clad arms
spread like a martyr's. Finches flitted

from the blaze to warble on her shoulders. She
    raised her hem

to show a padlock, her laughter bit
like a swarm of horseflies, she and the gown I'd
    bought exploded
into wet confetti.

I Lose My Wife to Christ

Just as Nance agreed our lives
were Porta-Potties clogged, just as she

agreed to dump
this house-tour reject and tow

the tent to Manitoba, you burst onto
Channel 12, wheelchair hubcaps

glinting, and like a fallen angel, right arm
tossing like a wind sock, flapped

a wing of your green robe
to show *God Loves Wealth*

When You Love Christ
stitched in gold, shouting how the more

we earn, the more baptisms we can buy
to clean up third-world

sties until *The World Is One*
for Him, and then you whapped the Bible crying

we deserve to trade our junkers in, trash
our shacks for flexi-stucco stuffed with leather

wraparounds, promising *Thirteen*
Ways the Lord Rewards.

Breakup

Wedding ring glistening in one
Dumbo-sized ear, John has ditched
his wife and kids—at the reading
last week I saw his boy toy unfolding
off the back of his bike and tonight

a woman is holding
his paw—plum lips
makeupless, chestnut hair sliding
off shoulders narrow
as the poof's are making me

crazy. Want her,
want him,
want John, don't care whose
arms, whose hungry
tongue give me reasons
to go on.

Listening to Bach's B Minor Mass

I hail the fifteen years he fidgeted,
yanking straight the curls of periwigs
to pour two hours of Kyrie, Gloria,
Credo, Sanctus, and Agnus Dei
into arias and five-part choruses thundering
toward insignificance
against the crash of collapsing
rubber trees, the hiss
of robot fingers jamming
axles into universal couplings—oh, cosmic
silence coming, earth gleaming
like a blue and white pot and no dreamers left
to piss peonies into it.

Life Force
—after Hal Larsen's painting

Torn green T-shirt running
for Mother's hugs against her boiling
breasts—violet block of Dad
twisting behind the wheel of his blue
Olds to blurt he cherished
me—my daughters flaring in pink,
Happy Birthday, Daddy. Oh, dominate
the black scribbles of today, arthritis
purpling my wrists, a white
river gnawing the longing to welcome
each tick of the clock I have left.

Giving Up

Not the results I thought, lipping off about
spiritual journey.

Bedding my wife mostly meant
catching her colds
and coughing them back—
unfolding a chair
for world peace on the capitol lawn?
Its struts iced my thighs.

Morphing into an old man knuckling away his
saliva, I've decided to celebrate
what is, the cat
birthing Siamese twins, eyes streaming
when I gaze at a moon
slated for aluminum silicate mining in twenty years.

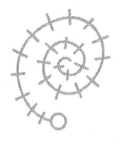

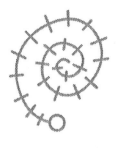

O
FRABJOUS
DAY

Emergency Plumbing Illustrated
—for Margaret

You rise and flush, a rusty
bridal veil bubbles out,
curse your ex, from a dresser
grab the book he wrote, fan
pages while your slippers sponge
the muck—you lift the porcelain top
and plunge into cold but the float
ball's arm won't budge. As you turn
to rush the phone, *Emergency
Plumbing Illustrated* flops
into the bowl, drowning proof
that young men still believe
they can save the world.

Learning How from Horned Toads

Gray as a day when nothing makes us laugh
though horned toads do their push-ups
under a moon so bright they think it sun,

a mood like ours would punish anyone
attempting jolly-jump-ups
to soothe a toddler racked by whooping cough

even though his grandma begged us off,
since sweating in our getups
breaks her rules of shower first, don't run

a gig into the ground. Oblivion spun
from rum-soaked butterups
won't save our boy from gagging even if

his cry can crack a coconut in half
and shatter both our teacups,
tempting us to fritter away the fun

envisioned for that hour when horned toads shun
the crusted hearts of grown-ups,
gray as days when nothing makes us laugh
under a moon so bright we think it sun.

Waking Up

Last night his wife untied the crimson
ribbon from her salt-and-pepper

ponytail and raised
the plum silk nightdress

he'd bought her. After years of
celebration beneath the flapping sheet, he only
    courts

thanksgiving,
but this morning his boxers strain again

as he pushes
through the florist's door—the hello

of the girl snipping stems
an oboe's, her nipples firm

as loganberries. With blossoms he intends
to buy, he longs to smother

this stranger, master her behind the counter
on potting soil whose wrapping he's ripped—

amazement shakes him like biting into aspirin.
    Clutching
a dozen sprays of hyacinth, he stumbles

into the sunshine, his staccato footsteps
scattering fragrance. But no one

pulls him over for driving
under the influence nor has he words for his wife's
    new

radiance as she follows him upstairs.

Prelude & Fugue XIX

His fingers cast sounds like seed, like rain,
like apricot petals. I stare
through the window at allergy-
laden junipers, drought-blackened
piñons—squirm thinking
how it smarts to sneeze
blood from my nose. How I loathe the dreariness
of rubbing sunblock in, its stench of rancid
butter recalling crawling
in vomit after downing tequila martinis
when I heard my sister wail
how her daughter collapsed from epileptic
heart failure. Like a blind man tearing
scabs off his eyes, the pianist's fingers spread
    painful
healing, and I'll badger anyone who'll listen
that Beethoven psychodramatizes,
Brahms sentimentalizes, Bartók
chips teeth but Bach is a periwigged
Tinkerbell touching my shame,

my wrinkled buttocks, this rush
of tasting anchovies, goat cheese, and a pear
for lunch, the warmth of my
arm around my wife
tonight—Bach pounds everything
into flour for sweet cakes, brings plump
huckleberries to dead vines, crystals
to cinder-smudged snow.

Okay, Cry, But Don't Forget Your Fiber

No wonder I'm trembling—

slaphappy I'll never need to press my ass
to an icy seat again.

Turn this damned electric blanket
up. Just because I can't
imagine Nothing
doesn't mean it's not there.

Rebirth

That scent—rose oil?
I'm going

to sneeze—stop carping,
she's home

kissing my ear—"Daddy,
so good"—my heart a puppy,

how many rathskellers has she closed down?
I smell tobacco,

why back now after
years in New York? Her cheek

pockets my tears, don't be
a sap, she wants money,

before she fled,
screamed me a fascist,

called her mother's boozing
my debt. I'd like to re-crib her,

buy her armfuls of jonquils—
damn you, Melinda, for unplugging the past.

Thursday Morning at Whole Foods Market

The film documentarian for whom recently she revealed
her plucked-lovebird childhood

hollos from the far end
of the meat counter. His teeth gleam like klieg lights,

brightening her now-that-my-husband's-
admitted-a-mistress-what-am-I-going-to-do?

But as she steps forward to order chicken,
invoking the courage to propose

coffee, he shouts, *You cut
in front of me,* blasting her

from the faux oak flooring
into a long ago

stare at Daddy who'd just slammed her
to her knees and stood sawing

razor wire across her reverence
with his *Don't you ever*

beg me to ditch a bottle. She grips the cart handle's
cold plastic but, gray bob

wagging, floats up close under the fluorescents
to gasp the conditioned air.

Different Waters

Coca-Cola's sweet snap drifts from a Big
Slurp cup spilled on the coffee

shop's black-and-white
terrazzo where Paul and Deena haul out

copies of *Heraclitus* they'll
discuss in group tomorrow. *As they*

step into the same river,
different waters

flow around them. Yesterday they munched
burgers, clinked cold

cans of Fresca. Now Victor, who at night pounds
his laptop

trading high-tech stocks,
stomps from behind the grill to plunge

a tattooed handful of hash browns into the garbage.
Dipping her pinky

into the honey, Deena thrusts it
at Paul. *Humans fail*

to be aware of what they do after
waking. Last week she dreamed of giving

birth to a daughter with the face
of a mole. The fry

dangling from a cardboard
plate drops to the tiles. Victor watches Deena finger

her tears away—suddenly she's
blubbering, hair spread like a willow. *Absent*

while present, Paul
mutters, jumping over to hold her. Victor's

cap bill bobs like a
duck's as he returns with a mop, smiling

because yesterday Microsoft soared.

Whirling has Worked for the Sufis Since 1273

This morning I spin in an overcoat
praying that CO_2 levels
high as when tyrannosaurs disappeared
don't slow the Gulf Stream,
sending us scrabbling into glaciers
for heat. Scientists portion ten thousand years
for our parades, ninety thousand for geysers
and blue ice, temperature swings
like bungee jumping off
roller coasters. Tomorrow I'll try gyrating
in bathing trunks. If enough of us
catch Destiny's attention, hey—
one man flapping his arms
can stop a train.

Nurturing

Stubbled jowls jiggling, pee
souring your slacks, do us a favor,
keel over in your swiveling recliner. Just die,

old-fart businessman yakking
to no one,

who taught me to fashion a Windsor knot
for my sixth-grade dance,
said you loved me instead of the paddling
I expected for C- in math—

don't die
just yet. Here comes Abbie gurgling
from her mother's hands, slaver

marking her path. As your Mona Lisa grin
stifles your chatter, a fist uncurls
from your thigh
and drops for the granddaughter

who mouths your forefinger
like a nipple.

Kate's Daydream

Now to wiggle St. Christopher
into the hole I just troweled—Chris, spread
your arms to stop traffic. Traffic?

mule-eared rabbits and mangy
coyotes—that white van from California
churning dust devils. *Willy, shout louder,*
somebody has to buy this dump

so I can haul you back
to Mendocino's cliffs and green
breakers to surprise me
from behind again, pull me against your overalls,

take me overlooking
the sea's thunder-roar and white spume.

Here mostly you slump
in the porch rocker while I bind
ponderosa needles for the basket kits
we hawk to museums. Like wind

in a cast-off chambered nautilus, *Willy,*
love me, Willy, I think this will do it,

St. Chris thigh-deep in caliche, the sun's
salt water cooling my collarbones.

War Again

and I'm flooded by a childhood
of cracking sand-crab shells,

popping kelp bulbs as I inch

bare-kneed over quartz,
sneaking beneath the umbrella
to feel my passed-out father's belly

rise and fall while his brother,

who once lobbed
death into German shallow-draft

landing craft, limps
toward the surf's sigh, Silver Star gleaming

from his shirt pocket—and scoops up
a starfish, waggling the corpse to show

how sun can make sequins
of salt-crusted knobs.

Having Exhausted Other Responses, We're

learning how to laugh. "That's pathetic"
creates a new aesthetic.

Who wants to listen to diabetics
pissing when hyenas can teach us
to howl?

Draftees

Soto at night pisses
blood on his poncho, refusing to enter

this hospital hot

as a jungle where Hedstrom's wrists seep,
Stone spews phlegm on his see-through

bib, black Thomas dry-retches

while his white nurse-wife massages
his scalp—myself, conscientious objector passing
    out

aspirin and stopcocking

morphine, soothing
as a songbird

gargling bleach, barring visions

of what's coming by recalling
sand fleas

hip-hopping off seaweed, polka-dotted

cheerleaders slapping their cheeks as the sun
lotioned their bodies
with sweat.

Mother's Daybook the Week Before She Died

Each line of the Queen's English,
a bar in her cage restraining the caterwauls
brawling to squeeze free—

a bicuspid's throb; a husband's
gibes; outrage that her son
ran from the wife she loved; knees
invaded by knives—

body wrapped in burlap shivering
in urine, soul

larking about waving a purple ribbon: *O Frabjous
Day*

Thumbing Our Noses

Pumping this stationary
bicycle to forestall
wheeling into a nursing home

up down up down bony pistons

makes me sweat—your white tennies
slapping the treadmill make me

gasp. Last night

tickling each other's
nipples with a feather, lemonade, Bach's
Wedding Cantata—your smile

outbeaming the moon.

Truffles and Castor Oil

Sprung from rehab, I kneel numb
as a man feeling the cold end of a pistol
pressing the back of his head, begging

God help me do Your will,
which seems bent, when I squint at the evening
    news,
on showing us how to dig mass graves

but when I brush the hair
of my wife, wounded
in her right shoulder during a break-in
at Longevity Café, that will seems bent on showing
    me
how to love. Confusion

that You could want
my happiness and our species' end
tempts me toward Wild Turkey territory

again—so I shake as though reprieved
and quake as though condemned, saddened
this new life roils my gut
like a bolted six-course meal at Four Seasons.

After Cryotransport, Lo ✓

I'll pay to freeze
my death in nitrogen, tympanic
probes in each ear canal, down
derry down to centigrade minus,
dry-ice cold with my
new family in stainless steel,
patient as robots
until nanomedicine pops us out
disease-free, hetero, homo,
or how we please, gawking at squawking
flocks of titanium ravens patrolling
dingy skies. Holy cerebrums
humming like combustion turbines
pushing our race beyond
three lifetimes—praise Him
from Whom all blessings flow.